BRIEFING
for the Board Room
and the Situation Room:
A Brief Guidebook

By Dr. Edward Mickolus
in association with The Analytic Edge

WANDERING
WOODS
PUBLISHERS

**Briefing for the Board Room and the
Situation Room: A Brief Guidebook**

By Edward Mickolus, PhD
in association with The Analytic Edge

First Edition 2015
Second Edition 2021

ISBN: 978-1-949173-08-6

Published in the United States by
Wandering Woods Publishers

Book Design, Cover and Typesetting by
Cynthia J. Kwitchoff (CJKCREATIVE.COM)

About the Authors

Edward Mickolus, PhD, is the President of Vinyard Software, Inc. He served a 33-year career with the Central Intelligence Agency, has written 40 books, and has taught intelligence tradecraft courses at numerous federal agencies. Vinyard Software's International Terrorism Data Center provides universities, research institutions, governments, the media, and others interested in international terrorism the best publicly-available data on terrorists and events around the world.

Jay Grusin, PhD, is the president of The Analytic Edge. He completed a successful 29-plus-year career at the Central Intelligence Agency in 2008. A member of the Senior Intelligence Service, he received the Distinguished Career Intelligence Medal in recognition of his contributions to the Agency. Widely recognized for his skills as an analyst, manager and teacher of analysts, Dr. Grusin helped create and deliver an analytic tradecraft course that redefined how it would be taught and formed the foundation of the Directorate of Intelligence tradecraft training curriculum. His company delivers intelligence training to a range of clients and has developed commercial applications to support decision making, focusing on helping to identify and manage/exploit uncertainty and risk.

Table of Contents

■ Introduction

Whatever your job, from attorney to intelligence officer, from doctor to financial analyst, and anything in between, at some point, you're going to be called upon to brief someone, whether it be your boss, colleagues, peers outside your organization, or someone outside your food chain but interested in your topic. This may require you to talk to someone one-on-one, to a large group in an auditorium, to a group via a video conference, or in hundreds of other scenarios.

This book is intended to give you the tools you need to succeed in briefing situations. We'll look at channeling your nervous energy, how to research an audience and the briefing environment ahead of time, how to organize the briefing and pepper it with effective graphics, how to answer questions, and how to put your individual speaking talents to their best use.

It's important to keep in mind that briefing is only a subset of general public speaking. Briefing is designed to convey information, often in what appears to be an informal, conversational setting, and often in a more structured setting. It does not include other forms of public speaking, be it delivering eulogies, performing standup comedy, or a plethora of other types of speaking. Some of the techniques relevant to briefing can be used in those scenarios, but for our purposes, we'll limit our discussion to informational briefings.

Briefing has its own unique requirements. It is a very specific subset of public speaking. Many of the audiences I've dealt with say that they find briefings preferable to written products. They've told me that in briefings:

- They can ask you questions.

- They can bounce ideas off you.

- They can get clarifications.

- They want to offer their views to you.

- They want to offer their praise and suggest ways they can support you.

- They want to give you additional tasking.

- They don't have time to read your paper but want the key points.

Despite your reservations about your skills, I know that you can succeed as a briefer. Consider when you introduce yourself to someone. You quickly summarize material that you've collected about yourself over the years, pick out the most important points, and present it in a well-organized, interesting presentation. That's all that briefing entails!

A Note on Terminology

Briefing: An information presentation, usually oral, sometimes festooned with handouts, slides, graphics, and other materials.

Principal: The senior-most individual who initially requested your presentation. Usually the most senior-ranking person in the room, but can sometimes be outranked by walk-ins who heard about your briefing.

Moat Monster: A gatekeeper for the principal, usually a special assistant (formerly known as a secretary, although special assistants do so much more in business and government), aide de camp, or executive assistant.

Minions: A great movie, but also refers to various aides to the principal. They can be equal to the principal in rank, or even senior to the principal if invited in after the principal secured the briefer's services.

■ Nervousness

In this chapter, we're going to examine reasons for and techniques that can be used to overcome stage fright, and help you to develop into a more confident speaker. We'll identify your personal reasons for nervousness, look at how you can embrace this source of energy and channel it into strengths, and develop methods to overcome nervousness based upon your individual needs.

Who among us is absolutely comfortable with any briefing situation? Who is somewhat nervous in certain public speaking/briefing situations? I know I am the second type. Jerry Seinfeld likes to cite the public opinion poll in which people ranked their fears. Death came in 7th. Public Speaking came in 1st. Which means that people would rather be in the casket than deliver the eulogy. Speaking of comedians, I tried standup for a while. I was surprised to learn how nervous my colleagues were. Even though they make it look easy, many of them threw up in the restroom before going on stage. This is not a solution I recommend, by the way, but it's useful for you to know that you can create a confident-seeming persona for an audience, no matter how nervous you may really feel.

What is it about public speaking/briefing that makes us nervous? Among the things my students have told me are fear of:

- making a fool of myself
- not being able to answer a question
- losing my place
- something going bad, not handling it well
- getting yelled at by the principal member of the audience/my boss/my colleagues

This general common theme of fear of something leads to a fear response, which entails a distinct set of **neuromuscular reactions**—the **fight or flight or freeze** syndrome. Your autonomic nervous system is getting ready to either run from danger or battle it head on. This shows up in the following symptoms, which starts with your brain's amygdala short-circuiting sensory information before the prefrontal cortex can process it. Instead, the amygdala registers danger and puts on hold the thinking part of your Mark 1 brain. Meanwhile, it kicks in the following symptoms:

- your heart races, pumping blood to your arms and legs and increasing your blood pressure
- blood is diverted from your fine motor groups that won't be of much use in the crisis (which is why your toes and fingers get cold and clammy) to your major muscle groups
- your spine gets cold for similar reasons
- your breath shortens while you try to get more oxygen into your lungs to assist this additional blood flow to your muscles
- your knees buckle, or knock, and your hands get tremors, because of being hit by all of this extra blood flow

- the adrenal glands release epinephrine and cortisol into the bloodstream
- your stomach reacts to all of this adrenaline by shutting down digestion, causing "butterflies"
- your tongue goes dry and throat muscles tighten because your system doesn't need fluid there
- you get goosebumps (when we were hairier, this lifted our hairs, making us look bigger to the perceived threat)
- you perspire, cooling you down in case you need to flee
- your eyelids widen and pupils dilate so that you can better see the threat
- your attention tunnel-visions
- while your brain is in emergency response mode, it shuts down other systems, such as those needed for short-term memory, concentration, and rational thought, which is why it's tough to get out your next words

Your body is ready—for something, even if you don't know quite what that something is. But your mind is still wondering—hey, body, what's going on here? Mind switching my other systems back on?

It's important to know that the audiences does not notice this. To them, you're fine. They're thinking about themselves, not you.

So how do we handle this fear—perhaps of the unknown?

One way is to **prepare**. The Boy Scouts have it exactly right here. Have an emergency plan. Control what you can control, and improvise if anything else comes up. Think about what might go wrong, and then figure out ahead of time what you would do. Listen to stories about the worst thing that happened to fellow briefers, and then conduct the following exercise: If that happened to me... what would I do?

For example, what would you do if

- **You can't remember your next point?** (Write down your key points on notecards. Even if you've prepped 50 times before murder boards, it's easy to blank when you're in the august presence of someone famous or powerful. Don't worry about how the audience will react to your checking out your note cards. A friend of mine was briefing a very senior official, when suddenly he couldn't remember his third point. The official said, "Son, I see a 1-2-3 on your notecards. Just read that bad boy to me!")

- **Your materials don't arrive?** (Bring Plan B backup material. Assume that materials can get lost in transit and have a few backups ready.)

- **Your briefing partner doesn't show?** (Know their material and have their handouts and notes with you. The audience probably knows that you were supposed to be a tandem team, and will appreciate your effort to fill in. They've been there before.)

- **The principal says they have only 5 minutes, and you brought an hour's worth of material?** (Look at your key points and topic sentences of major paragraphs. What's the most important thing that you want them to know? Tell them that. Period.)

Consider as well the **advantages** that you have as the briefer. Keep in mind:

- Management chose me to represent the group. They're in my corner.

- I'm the most knowledgeable (and maybe the smartest) person in the room—at least on this subject. You weren't asked to talk about something you don't know.

- If I don't know something, I have the backing of the most knowledgeable organization in the world on this topic. Use "**we** believe" language.

- The principal and rest of the audience wants me to succeed, as they're counting on me to guide them through the data. They don't want me to fail.

- Everyone in the room has been where I am now, and will empathize/understand if I slip up.

That *intellectually* channels our nervousness. But that doesn't mean that our stressed-out body is buying what our rational brain is telling us. Let's try a few *physical* techniques to back up the reasonable approach. Here are a few relaxation techniques, some of which will require a partner:

Breathe deeply. Turn down the lights. Close your eyes. Breathe in for a count of 3, hold for a count of 3, breathe out for a count of 3. Repeat 4 times.

Guided Imagery/Visualization. Have a partner slowly read to you a relaxing passage describing, say, a dock on a quiet lake. They can read a text, or ad lib based upon the following talking points (hey! They're briefing!)

- Walk slowly around the dock and notice the colors and textures around you.

- Spend some time exploring each of your senses.

- See the sun setting over the water.

- Hear the birds singing.

- Smell the pine trees.

- Feel the cool water on your bare feet.

- Taste the fresh, clean air.

Progressive muscle relaxation. Tighten your eyes, then relax. Repeat this through eyes, nose, lips, shoulders/neck, diaphragm, fists, legs, toes. If you have time, you can also go through a more robust series, including:

- Right foot
- Left foot
- Right calf
- Left calf
- Right thigh
- Left thigh
- Hips and buttocks

- Stomach
- Chest
- Back
- Right arm and hand
- Left arm and hand
- Neck and shoulders
- Face

Some **coping mechanisms** are specific to the individual, and might work for you. Some students have tried the following, keyed to their interests:

- I like to **shake hands** with every member of the audience, thus developing a connection (albeit fleeting) with them and letting me fool myself into thinking that they are acquaintances who are on my side.

- **Visit** the room. Get sight lines, lay of the land, where you will sit/stand, where the audience will be, lighting, acoustics, who will introduce you, and anything else that comes to mind that will make you feel that the room belongs to you.

- **Smile**—it calms the audience, and you.

- Some students **laugh** out loud (again, try this in private, not the briefing room). It releases tension.

- **Visualize** the audience as being on your team.

- **Feed off the audience's energy.** There are always smilers in the audience. Initially aim your eye contact at them, then expand your eye contact to the rest of the room.

- Bring **note cards**. You'll feel calmer if you know that they're there in case you get a brain cramp.

- Some students talk a **walk**—or **run**—burning off the excess energy. This does not mean that you can run away from the briefing entirely! It is ok, however, to move during the briefing.

- **Close your eyes**, say "I am relaxed," before going on.

- Release tension with unobtrusive **isometric** exercises—crinkle your toes, make fists, release air with a deep cleansing breath.

- Relax your voicebox. Morgan Freeman, a gifted "voice," advocates **yawning** (again, before, not during the briefing. Yawning is way too infectious to do this in front of an audience. One of the most virulent aspects of life is yawning 3 seconds after you see someone else do it! You don't want to give them permission to yawn by serving as a role model!). I drink only room temperature water. Any other temperature attacks your vocal cords. Do this before your presentation.

- Be **conversational**. Many students say they prefer to answer questions rather than rattle on. So say to yourself, "I was just asked a question. My next paragraph perfectly answers it." You can sometimes salt rhetorical questions into your presentation to get people wondering what the answer will be, and further focus their attention on your presentation.

- If you are in a situation that permits PDAs, listen to soothing **music**.

- **Visualize** that you've successfully completed the briefing and that things went well.

- A karate black belt who also briefs hides in the restroom, doing three high kicks and four fast punches before going on stage.

- I walk to the lectern/podium, blink twice, and tell myself that the nervousness is Star Wars' **The Force,** which can be channeled to my liking. The extra energy lets me be an animated speaker, with gestures, facial expressions, and changes in pitch and volume as appropriate.

What **techniques have you tried that worked** for you? What other techniques have you heard about? Maybe they'll work for you.

■ Know Your Audience

In this chapter we'll examine the difference between "briefing to" and "briefing about," look at the topics you should cover in researching a customer, how to find material relevant to tailoring the briefing to specific customer needs and expectations, and avoid unforced errors of organizational norms/etiquette.

All briefing opportunities are unique. I've addressed thousands of groups and individuals over the years and no two audiences are alike. Always keep in mind that you are briefing Audience A on topic X. You are NOT "giving the topic X briefing to Audience A." It's crucial to tailor your remarks, slides, and handouts for your audience's job needs and background.

For the next 30 minutes, try researching an individual you will be briefing soon. (Don't worry. I'll still be here when you return.) Focus on the following considerations:

- Biography
- Requirements of the job
- General level of knowledge about the topic

- Bias/experiences regarding the topic, your organization, and you

- Other sources of information on this topic

- Why you are in the room with this individual (is a meeting/negotiation coming up, is a decision to be made, are they going on a trip, is there a crisis/new development, have they read your paper)

- How they like getting information

Welcome back. I bet that you've found a lot of information, even in just half an hour. Let's walk our way through this data, concentrating on:

- What sources did you use?

- Was there conflicting information? How did you resolve these conflicts?

- How reliable were these sources?

- How would this piece of audience background affect how you organize and deliver the briefing?

There are other sources you might try:

- Who knows the principal and can give you tips?

- Have the principals written anything?

- Have the principals given speeches?

- Does your organization have a representative embedded in the principal's organization?

- What does the organization's website say about the principal?

- Are there others who have served with them, went to senior schools with them?

- Is there a Wikipedia entry on them? Can you track down the sources cited in the Wikipedia entry?

- Is there an official resume?

- Does someone in your management chain or extended network know them?

Sometimes we have the luxury of getting a heads-up about a briefing, and have time to research the topic and the audience. Sometimes you get the call, "come to the boardroom, NOW!"

After the initial shock has worn off, ask yourself: What to do? What sources could you use if you have no time to prepare, and walk into their anteroom cold? You might consider:

- chatting up the secretary/concierge
- talking to staffers
- looking at their I-love-me wall and their desk clutter
- noting their calendars to see what they've just heard and what's coming up that might be the backstory for your tasking

Beyond what you already found out in your research about this individual, you will have **Other Concerns,** including:

Forms of Address

- How does the individual like to be addressed (not how does your organization handle titles)? Sir, ma'am, your highness, Senator sound fine to us, but are there minefields you should know about? For example, how does a military officer address a senior woman? "Ma'am." That's fine for the military culture. But sometimes it can be misinterpreted. Senator Barbara Boxer once famously stopped a senior military officer who had ma'am'd her, asking to be called by her title. These titles can be very important to the principal, and can give you an inkling of how the briefing can be tailored. For example, in the CIA, everyone addresses each other by first name (often because we don't actually know each other's real name!). This can sound very informal to outsiders, but is the culture of the organization. On the other hand, some principals like a previous title. Even though they might now be a Director, they might prefer General, or Senator, or Judge, or whatever else they were. Even if they earned their Doctorate decades ago and haven't used it since, they might like to be called Doctor. (One more cultural thing at CIA, however: Only MDs are called Doctor. All the rest are first-named.) Look to the principal's staffers for guidance on what's appropriate from a briefer. Don't just accept "Oh, I'm on a first-name basis with him." "Yes, but I'm not (yet). What should I call him?"

- How does the principal tend to address briefers? Can you get tagged with a nickname/epithet? Are they condescending? In awe? Friendly? Aloof? Does this treatment vary by their moods/what's happening in their world today?

Kinesics

- Does the principal like to shake hands (and if so, how hard—you might encounter a bonecrusher trying to establish dominance in the room, but also don't be put off by a limp wrist)? Follow their lead on handshakes—if they don't offer their hand, it could be that they are ill, and don't want to infect you.

- Is there a cultural taboo about touching?

- Is the principal a hugger, or someone who taps your shoulder or knee when making a point? In formal American office cultures, such behavior can easily throw you off your game.

- By the way, make sure that you aren't so invested in ensuring that you sit in your assigned chair that you obliviously walk right past the extended hand of your principal.

Room Energy

- Does the principal enjoy give-and-take, using your briefing as a springboard to discussion?

- Does the principal prefer to read in silence, then ask questions?

- Does the principal want to hear you brief and not read?

- Has the principal received a copy of your briefing notes/accompanying materials beforehand, and thus want to jump right into a discussion? Just because you sent the material ahead of time does not mean that the moat monsters shared it with him, and/or that he had time to read it before you showed up.

Minions

- Will there be straphangers?

- Are they cleared for any sensitive material you might discuss?

- How many of them are there?

- Consider all of the other questions we asked about principals. You might want to know some of the answers to those questions regarding the assistants.

Medical issues

Does the principal have:

- A hearing problem (some principals will turn their good ear toward you. Sometimes that loss of eye contact can be off-putting to a briefer.)

- A fleeting illness

- Colorblindness

- A tendency to rest their eyes (Do not confuse closed eyes with sleep. Many senior principals close their eyes to attend more carefully to your words, without visual distractions.)

When I was your age... (institutional memory)

- Does your organization keep records of how briefings went?

- Can you easily find this type of information on recorded tribal memory?

- If not, can you easily find individuals who have dealt with the principal, who can give you tips?

Finally, what is the **culture of briefings at the recipient organization**? I've found that styles differ between, say, the military, CIA, FBI, DEA, boardrooms, and academe. Some organizations expect you to bring PowerPoints, and will be put off if you don't come armed with same. Some organizations have subcultures, with very different expectations of the role and style of successful briefers. Some expect slides, some abhor them. You can easily lose your audience if you inadvertently break one of these unwritten rules.

■ Know Your Environment

In this chapter, we will explore how to prepare for what might go wrong given the environment in which we'll be briefing, develop a toolbox with all sorts of Plan B ideas, and help you build confidence in knowing that you can handle unexpected reverses.

A key source of nervousness is our uneasy feeling that something can go wrong—we're not sure what—and that we won't be prepared and look foolish. Here are a few things that have gone wrong in my and my friends' briefings that didn't have to do with the substance of the briefing or the audience. Stated differently: "I wish I'd known ahead of time…"

- Gestured too broadly, hit the principal's coffee cup, doused him with scalding hot coffee. Do you then help clean up their laps?

- Audiovisual system and/or computer didn't work; host's systems incompatible with our DVDs/CDs; no/spotty Internet connection

- Slides/DVD didn't arrive

- Handouts didn't arrive
- Trapped in restroom when door handle fell off
- Elevator jams, trapping briefer
- Many more people in the room than expected; didn't have enough handouts
- Had to stand very far away from the principal, who was the only person in the room with briefer
- Weather/car splatter ruined briefer's attire
- Rain/snow/sleet damaged handouts/technical equipment for briefing
- Last-minute demand for briefer, who had dressed for Casual Day; no time to go home to change
- Security officers refused to allow briefers to take tech equipment into building
- Microphone too loud/soft/staticy/nonexistent
- Loud drilling/other construction noise nearby
- Not enough paper for the flip chart
- No markers for the flip chart
- Laser pointer's batteries died
- Unknown people walking in and out during briefing
- Birds/animals entering/leaving briefing room
- Sun in briefer's eyes
- Chair/table broke during briefing (my favorite—three briefing team members leaned back too far on a couch, tipping it backwards, spilling them)

How can you protect yourself? Here's a simple truism that briefers too often forget: briefings occur somewhere, and those "somewheres" are unique. Those "somewheres" present unique challenges, some of which we cannot control, but many of which we can, if we act ahead of time. Sometimes we're on our turf, sometimes the principal's, sometimes on a neutral court.

What can you do ahead of time to prevent disaster?

If you can, get into the briefing room beforehand—ideally, before the day of the briefing as well as an hour before the briefing—and use the above litany as a checklist. Among the considerations:

- **sightlines** Will the sun be in your eyes? Can you see the audience so that you can call on them if they have a question? Can they see you? Are there obstructed views?

- **sound**—not just "Is there a microphone?" but "how do I quickly find A/V staff onsite if things go wrong?" Check the acoustics of the room. Can they hear you? Will you be able to hear their questions?

- Are there any **security** requirements that limit your flexibility? How much time does the security staff need to check out your equipment, and you? If you're in a classified environment, have your clearances arrived ahead of time? If you're hosting the briefing, has your security staff received the clearances of the audience members?

- Do you need to pass **credentials** ahead of time?

- Is the A/V equipment **compatible** with your computer/PDA?

- What **language** will the briefing be in? Meet with the translator ahead of time and explain uncommon technical terms.

- What's the **dress** code? Don't just mimic their putative style. What do they expect from someone from your organization briefing someone from their organization?

- What's the **organizational culture regarding briefings**? Do they demand slides? Just because your organization doesn't do PowerPoint doesn't mean that military officers will be comfortable sans slides. Sales staff might need charts and graphs.

- Where are you supposed to **sit**? In some organizational cultures, the principal sits in the middle of the table, rather than at the end. Make sure that you know your place, literally.

- **What's the principal look like?** Find a photo. You want to make sure that you're addressing the right person. A colleague once began addressing the best-dressed person in the room, only to be stopped and introduced to the scruffier, but more powerful, principal.

- Are you using a **tablet**? Only, or with other materials? With a projector? Are you going to hand it to the principal? How are you going to ensure that what you want to be clicked, gets clicked? Are there security concerns about tablets in the room? Is there glare?

After you've considered all of these items, go back to the original horror stories and ask yourself how your pre-briefing preparation can assist you in avoiding, or at least mitigating, these mishaps.

This will give you some feeling for what you should consider before you walk into a briefing. Other things can happen but at least you know that you can still get through surprises by being flexible and being willing to switch to Plan B seamlessly. Briefing is all about thinking on your feet, even if you're sitting.

■ Organizing a Briefing

In this chapter, we'll examine how to develop an effective substantive presentation in which you articulate the key point—takeaway—of the briefing, state that takeaway as a Bottom Line Up Front (BLUF), organize the briefing using an inverted pyramid, provide supportive information in correct order, and develop an effective closing.

The key to briefing is keeping in mind that it is a briefing. It is not a declamatory reading of your paper. It is not a public speaking exercise to persuade, or entertain, or do any of the other types of speaking opportunities listed by, say, Toastmasters or a public speaking course. It is to inform policymakers and guide them through the relevant information on a topic. While there is some overlap between generic public speaking and briefing—more so as the audience expands in number and diversity—there are specific tradecraft techniques that you can master to become an effective briefer.

Where to start?

There are numerous types of briefings, including:

Tabletop: You sit across a desk or conference table with a principal and perhaps his aides. This is the most common scenario, and easier to control, because you usually have a heads-up and have time to prepare.

Informal: in which the principal, often your boss or colleague, asks for a quick update.

Impromptu/Elevator: Often you're literally in the elevator when the principal walks in and says, "so, what are you working on?" You do not want to say, "Nothing much." Always have 3 key points ready to go. Variations include walking down the hallways, eating in the cafeteria when the boss suddenly wants to join you, or getting a tap on your shoulder while at your desk.

Walkabout: At times, the principal wants to get out of the office and/or has to go to another meeting, to his car, etc. It's up to you to keep pace with him, making your points while ensuring that others who should not hearing the substance of your briefing are excluded. In rare cases, this can be a running briefing—General David Petraeus liked to have his briefers join him for 6-mile runs. And he was fast!

Group: You are one of several briefers on a panel.

Conference: This is similar to an academic Address to the Academy, in which you have scores or perhaps hundreds of people in front of you. Variations include congressional testimony and press conferences.

Remote: Sometimes you'll have occasion to speak during a video teleconference or other times via a multi-phone telephone conference.

No matter what the type of briefing, your key question should be: Why are you in the room? What is the **purpose** of the briefing? The principal is asking the same question; they deal with dozens of individuals each day, and might have forgotten why you were invited. Remind them. "You asked _____. I'm here to report that _____." Are you informing a non-specialist audience, are you providing updates on a fast-moving situation, are you offering analysis of a complex situation, outlining alternative scenarios and opportunity analysis?

Keep in mind that (for purposes of this paragraph) this is your briefing. Do not use someone else's slides, talking points, or other materials. They were created by/for someone else to deliver to a different audience.

Paradoxically, keep in mind that it is also the audience's briefing, and it can go in a direction that they find helpful to them, but derails your carefully-prepared/memorized outline.

Ask yourself: **what does the audience already know**? How much can I assume? At what level of knowledge should I conduct the briefing? The latter question is particularly important if your briefing is of a technical nature. "Technical" can have a very broad meaning, even if you're looking at political issues. Some audiences may care deeply about street-level political issues in the 4th most populous village in Mauritius. Others might need a map of the Indian Ocean just to place Mauritius, or even the Indian Ocean. Keep in mind that your audience might be experts, but just not experts on your topic.

Once you have decided what type of briefing you are giving, think about your **thesis statement**—the main point you want to make. This thesis is stated up front in the introduction, again in the body, and once more in the conclusion. Vary the wording, but the main thesis should be repeated three times (or more in a long briefing).

Stated differently, what is the **key analytical point** of the briefing? If you could leave the audience with only one sentence, what would that be? If the interlocutor asked a specific question, what is the straightforward answer? This is your opening sentence, your **Bottom Line Up Front** (BLUF). What has changed and why does it matter to the principal? All else in the briefing will flow from this.

Then ask yourself: What **other key points** do I need to make? Organize these as you would topic sentences for paragraphs. This becomes your **Roadmap**. After you blurt out the BLUF, you want to share with the audience your roadmap for the briefing. This should be offered in the language of a **menu** ("I'm prepared to discuss A, B, and C today."), vice dictating a set-in-stone agenda ("I'm going to cover A, B, and C, in that order."). The first formulation subtly tells the audience that if they want to hear about C first, you're willing to jump ahead to C. They'll interrupt you anyway; you might as well at least be gracious about it up front.

What should these key points cover?

Former Secretary of State Colin Powell used to say: "Tell me what you know, what you don't know, how sure you are, and what it means." So be sure to include:

What is known

- What happened
- Why
- The impact so far
- The Key Question
- Separate facts from judgments
- Delineate your levels of confidence. Gauge the level of certainty—how good is our sourcing, what is their/its access, is there denial and deception going on
- What are we doing to fill our knowledge gaps?

What is ahead—Outlook

- Draw inferences
- Identify and test key assumptions

- Determine key drivers and vulnerabilities
- What if you're wrong?

Identify the most likely outcome. From there, derive:

- Implications
- Opportunity analysis (not policy prescriptions)
- Mitigation strategies (if there is no opportunity, how do we at least clean up?)

Consider other **alternatives**.

Identify indicators—what to watch for.

You don't need to cover all of these in your presentation, but have these points in your back pocket in case the audience raises a question about how you came to your conclusions.

From there, develop the key points, using a **pyramid style.** Start with the key point, then use supplementary data, leading with your strongest data bits. This is the reverse of classical academic style, which shows the data, how it was analyzed, and only then reveals the conclusion—along with a plea for further research and research grants!

A few simple hints

You are writing talking points designed to help you to speak, not to read silently. Writing for reading a paragraph in a book is not the same as writing for saying out loud. What this means is that

- Your **sentences should be shorter**. You need to breathe, and your audience needs time to process what you began with at the start of your sentence until you ultimately meander up to the period that ends the sentence.

- You should check for **tongue-twisters.** You can do this only by **practicing aloud**—you will not be able to spot tongue-twisters by reading the text silently to yourself.

- Memorize your opening 3 sentences—your name/office/
account, BLUF, menu. This gives you eye contact, initially establishing your credibility in the all-important initial
minute.

You have now developed a tightly-focused briefing that
covers all of the material the audience needs. But how do you
help them remember what you say?

There are a host of memory tricks, many of them articu-
lated by the Heath brothers' *Made to Stick*. Their simple mne-
monic is SUCCESS:

Simple

Unexpected

Concrete

Credible

Emotional

Story

All of which leads to **Success**

Simple is not simplistic. Our audiences are intelligent, but
might not have the background in our topic that we do. Do
the intellectual heavy lifting for them. Don't burden them with
jargon and obscure acronyms. Just state your message in plain
English, a dialect not often heard in academe, government or
corporate boardrooms.

- "We are losing our market share to competitor X because
we do not offer these 3 features that our customers say
they want."

- "We are losing the war because we do not have sufficient
support from our allies in the following 3 areas."

If you have to explain a technical term, do so. But make
sure that the audience is not already au courant with the term.

A friend once was briefing an admiral, and found himself saying, "a DSV, that's a Deep Submersible Vehicle" before being interrupted by, "Son, I was a submarine driver. I know what a DSV is!"

Unexpected breaks a pattern. Major breakthroughs in product development, idea generation, and innovation can be directly traced to shifting assumptions, or simply stating something differently than everyone else does. Try a different way of arraying your data in a presentation. An economist, rather than offering a dizzying array of numbers, might say, "I'd like to defuse several myths which have grown up around this topic."

Concrete gives examples easy to understand. Numbers, especially of high magnitudes, can be difficult to grasp. What does a nanosecond mean? Admiral Grace Hopper, inventor of the term "computer bug", calculated how far light travels in a nanosecond (11½ inches), then handed 11½-inch strips of copper wire to every member of her audience. I still have mine. This makes it memorable. Give them examples, not abstracts. If you can show them props, even better. And if you can give them a takeaway prop that reminds them of your key message, it's likely that they'll share it with people who were not in the briefing room with you. "Concrete" can be the briefer's strongest force multiplier.

Credible Psychologists will tell you that eye contact is the #1 determinant of whether the audience believes you. After that, it can't hurt to have credentials relevant to the topic. Have you been to the area of discussion? Do you work on the topic? Have you published on it? Does your team have decades of experience on it? Do you speak the local language(s)? You are not trying to say, directly, "I'm the expert on this," as this only baits the audience into challenging you to a game of stump the chump. "Ok, expert. How many precincts does New Delhi have?"

Emotional links the topic to the audience's experience, previous, current, or future. "Here's what you're going to experience when you go here." What's in it for them (WIIFM)? "Here are three issues that are going to be occupying your in-box in the next week."

Story: We're hardwired to understand stories. Aesop's fables are told in story form, and we all remember the morals of those stories. The Bible is told in parables—stories. The Gospels did not just say "go ye forward and be good." They instead offered "Jesus was at a wedding and here's what happened." If you can weave a story that offers cultural touchstones that will resonate with your specific audience, so much the better. "This country's history is similar to what happened in your state in 1860-1890."

Finishing up

If you see that your time is up (the principal is standing, putting on his/her coat, is usually an indicator; the scheduler saying "your next appointment has arrived" is another), you have several options for finishing:

- Ask if they have any questions
- Summarize your key point
- If there's something you didn't cover that you really should, say, "I'd be remiss if I didn't leave you with the following insight…"

Now that you've written it, rehearse, in front of an audience. I'd suggest not doing it in front of a mirror. The only person you will not see in the briefing room is you, so why practice against that audience? Have a murder board—it can be just one person—listen to the briefing, make presentation suggestions, and ask you questions. It'll increase your confidence, and better prepare you.

Other Best Practices

- **Number your note cards/sheets.** In case you drop them, you can quickly put Humpty back together again.

- **Write your notes in large font.** 12-point Palatino is fine for reading the newspaper, but not for letting you find your next point. 24-point is better.

- **Prepare 3 briefings:** one of the length originally stated by the scheduler, one an elevator-style one-minute briefing in case your principal says s/he has to run; and an hour of supplementary material in case the principal finds you and the topic fascinating. All of these scenarios will eventually play out during your briefing career.

■ Graphics

In this chapter we will take a look at some best practices of briefings, and some popular-but-inept practices. We will discuss how to use graphics as supplements to briefings, not as loss-leaders, consider how to design graphics, and how to correctly use slides, briefing notes, and handouts.

How often do you use graphics in your presentations? How often have you seen them correctly used by others? How about ineptly used? I'm guessing that you've seen more inept than correct uses.

Let's examine how to use graphics—visual aids, including maps, photos, charts, and other images—to enhance your presentation. Bottom line up front: you run the briefing, not PowerPoint!

Here are a few simple distinctions:

- **Slides**, whether in PowerPoint or other software, can be useful visual aids as supplements to your briefing, but only as supplements. PowerPoint is a tool, not the show.

- The **Notes Pages** of PowerPoint can be helpful to you in keeping track of what you want to say. They should not be on the slide per se. You are not reading the slide as your notes, nor are you reading the slide along with the audience, or worse, to the audience.

- **Handouts** are separate supplements. You can provide the audience with as much material as you want. You can send the handouts as read-aheads if appropriate. Sometimes, your briefing is a result of a paper you wrote about which the audience has questions. Sometimes, they are read-heres—something the audience needs right now to follow along.

As is the case in your writing, visual aids, often called graphics, can be helpful in getting your message across to your audience. They make facts or figures easier to grasp, underscore a point, and add variety.

Not all visual aids work. Some can undercut your message by distracting the audience. Avoid ones that are cluttered, outdated, not suitable to your purpose, or irrelevant to the message being conveyed.

Where to begin?

Here's a major secret that no one has shared with you. There are no magic numbers. There is no magic number of slides to use. There is no magic number of bullet points to put on a slide (although when cornered, I'd say it's One). There is no magic number of words to put on a slide, although the fewer the better. In his TED talks for product releases, Steve Jobs was known to use hundreds of slides. His secret was that he didn't burden you with text. He just showed images. Jobs's presentations were generally praised as being memorable, even inspiring. Don't use text if you don't have to; use images.

Go back to the points you want to make. What is your **key message**? What are the supplementary points? What are the individual pieces of data that support those points? In each case, is there a visual that can illustrate that point?

If it's an **image**, sans words, great. This technique is called Presentation Zen, which you'll find on your reading list.

If you don't have an image per se, what are the **fewest words** you need that can convey this message? Can you include a photo/graphic with the words?

You have several tools to use here:

- **Maps**—Make sure they are easy to read and the places on the map that you are referring to are well-marked and visible to the audience. Simplicity is key—if you have more material on a map than is necessary to make your point, it can too quickly distract the audience. You want to guide their eyes to what's important; you don't want their eyes to wander to other locales on the map.

- **Charts and graphs**—A chart or graph on a page of text may be fine, but might not transfer to a large screen or Power Point projection. For example a pie chart does not often transfer directly from the printed page to a large visual aid because many times the writing as you go around the chart is upside down. Keep your charts and graphs simple. Avoid clutter and make your charts and graphs easy to read.

- **Photographs**—Photos make excellent visual aids. If you are talking about individuals, photos of them can help the audience retain the points you are making. Satellite photography, say, Google Earth, is often a big hit with an audience. Highlight what you want them to remember.

Do not let your visual aids compete with what you are saying. Make the point you want to make orally and then stop talking so that the audience can intellectually process the visual aid and integrate it with what you just said. If you talk through the visual aid, or leave the visual aid up too long, your words will compete with what the audience is seeing. Remember: although you've practiced this briefing several times, this is the first time that the audience has heard this information presented in this order, in quite this way. Give them time to think about it.

Fonts

Fonts come in two flavors: serif'd and sans serif'd.

> **Serif:** includes a small line attached to the
> end of a stroke in a letter or symbol
>
> **Sans Serif:** does not use those lines

You can use one of each on your slide—although remember to keep it down to just a few words—but make sure that the fonts are designed to be used together. Titles can be in sans serif; quotations can be in serif. Text in an article is usually in serif.

Be sure to use a "professional"-looking font—no Jokerman (or Comic!), no hard-to-read *italicized* font.

> This is French Script
>
> *This is hard to read.*
>
> This is cool, but still hard to read.
>
> What were they thinking when
> they designed these fonts?

Color can highlight your key message, setting it off from the background. Just remember to use contrast—don't put a blue text on a blue background. Find out if your principal is color blind. If so, be careful with red/green contrast, which is the major type of color blindness in men. Try to avoid intense, bright colors. Lean toward gentler hues.

What not to include:

Chartjunk—You don't need your company's/organization's logo on every single slide. Show it on the first slide, with your name. After that, give the audience credit for remembering you and the organization. You can always give them a business card, read-aheads, and other handouts that are replete with your team colors. Do not use them on your slides—they just draw the eye away from your message.

Cool effects, including fade-ins, clip-art, animation, blinking words, multiple colors, fly-ins, multiple fonts, drop shadows, watermarks, and anything else that distracts from your message. If the audience thinks "that's really cool. I wonder how the briefer did that," it's a distraction and they're no longer thinking about what you're saying. Just because you can do something does not mean that you should do it. Just because you recently learned something cool in a PowerPoint course does not mean that you now have license to subject your audience to the technique. If it helps your message, fine. If not, leave it out. Do not force the audience to do the intellectual heavy lifting by taking their eye off the ball.

Lots and lots of material on one slide. Military briefers especially like to do this. It is not a sign of competence to try to snow the audience with a blizzard of information on a single slide. Let them savor the single idea. They might actually remember it. They will not remember beaucoup details. Lawyers will often tell you that if they have 10 great arguments, the jury will remember none of them. Concentrate on what's important.

Typos. Proofread. Proofread again. Have someone else proofread it. If you have an inveterate editor like me in the audience, you'll lose your audience's attention—and their confidence in your competence—with such unforced errors.

How often have you suffered through listening to someone **read their slides** to you? In addition to being condescending—you're perfectly capable of reading—it also generates cognitive dissonance. Your Mark One Brain translates visual text into auditory information. But when you're also hearing that information—at a different pace from the speed at which you read—your brain is essentially hearing it twice. This is the same effect as when you have a film's translation poorly-synchronized.

You can move from 2D presentations (slides and handouts) to 3D—props, which are particularly effective if you can pass them around to kinesthetic learners. You can demonstrate—physically—how the item works. You can let the audience try it.

A few simple tips

- The fewer words on a slide, the better.

- One idea per slide.

- You're not being charged by the slide, so if you have to use a batch of slides to make your points, fine. The rule of thumb is fewest words, not fewest slides.

- Make sure your text is large enough to read, and your photos/graphics are big enough to see, from the back of the room.

- When in doubt, go with a graphic vs. tabular rows/columns of numbers.

- Remember how Americans' eyes move on a page: left-right, top-bottom, big-little, bright-dark.

- Use visuals pictorially—Graphs, pictures of equipment, maps, flow charts, and bar graphs provide insight that might require many words.

- Titles should be in the same position on the page, using the same color, font, and size.

Handouts

You can put as much or as little material in a handout as you want, but there's one simple rule to remember: Don't give audience the handouts **until you're ready for the audience to read them**. What do you tend to do when you receive a handout? You immediately drop your eyes away from the speaker and begin reading, hoping to get ahead of the speaker. If you want 'em to read it then, fine. If you don't, hold on to the handouts.

Handouts, however, are **Not your slides**. Do not give them your slides. If you've done your slides correctly, they're simple images with very short text. This is not going to be enough for them to get your points if they did not attend your briefing. For those who were not in the room, give them something that's written to be read, not heard and seen in person. With handouts, you can lose their eyes, or guide their eyes. Make sure the timing works for you.

■ How to Answer Questions

In this chapter, we'll discuss types of questions and how to answer them in a positive, professional manner. You'll develop confidence in handling any type of question, friendly or hostile, expected or unexpected, gentle or difficult. You'll find tips on how to analyze likely issues to be raised by the principal and prepare responses, apply suggested styles of responses, and lessen fear-of-the-unknown-question nervousness.

We can prepare for what we're going to say, if not interrupted. But how do we prepare to answer questions and other interruptions when we don't know what the audience is going to ask? This can be the source of nervousness—we don't want to stammer and look foolish while trying to formulate an answer.

Let's take a look at the types of questions, and situations, you'll face.

The majority of your questions will be **well-considered** and build upon what you've conveyed. Your interlocutor will be seeking insights about what's going on, and looks to you to **guide them through the data**. What it all means to them, what's going to happen next, what they can do to affect outcomes are typically on the top of their agendas. While you'll probably organize your briefing to handle these issues, you might be interrupted by an audience eager to jump ahead to the "so what" portion of your briefing.

The key thing for you to keep in mind—whose briefing is it? Yours or the audience's? Who is the most important person in the room? You or the principal? The principal. You're there to help the principal. Don't put them off by saying "we'll get to that later" or "Please hold your questions till the end." What do you think when you hear those replies? As soon as you say that, you irritate the audience, and they won't hear anything else that you say until you somehow stumble across the answer to their question downstream. You've now wasted goodwill and the attention of your audience.

Listen to the entire question. Don't interrupt. Don't assume you know what they have in mind. Don't talk over them.

Rather, give them a **concise answer up front**. Sometimes all they're looking for is a simple "yes" or "no". Try that. If they want an expansion on how you got to that conclusion, they'll prompt you for it. Pause to give them time to ask a follow-up. If they do not, return to where you were by using a connector such as "and that leads us to…" or "as I was saying…" Do not give them the impression that they are needlessly interrupting you. You want them to have ownership of what they are saying, and to process the information at their own pace and style.

If you're temporarily stuck for the answer, focus on the forehead of a person in the 3rd row. This looks like eye contact to the audience, involves them, and makes you look thoughtful. The idea will eventually come to you. It also couldn't hurt to check your note cards at this point. You might also want to restate/clarify the question, buying time.

What do you do if you **don't know the answer**? Here's your new best friend. After eye contact, the second most important aspect of establishing credibility with the audience is your willingness to admit that you don't know everything. It feels odd, after having gone through graduate school oral defenses, where we're expected to have snappy answers to anything on the tips of our tongues, to say, "I don't know." But these simple words also tell the audience that you're confident in everything you've said up to that utterance, and are not attempting to snow them. Say it with me right now: **"I don't know."**

Crucial to using this phrase, however, is bringing in its cousin, **"and I'll get back to you with an answer."** To underscore that point, write down the question in front of the audience. It tells them that you take them seriously, and will, in fact, get them an answer. They'll let you know if idle curiosity was behind the question, or if they really would appreciate your following up. Make sure that you *do* follow up.

Treat every opportunity to respond to a customer's question you could not answer during the briefing as a chance to develop or maintain an important relationship. Briefings should not be viewed as one-offs. Keep the relationship going. You want a long-term customer. Keep giving them what they need/want.

In your prep work, you should do some background reading on sidebar issues related to your topic. If, say, you are briefing on the Peruvian economy, expect questions on Peruvian leaders and Peruvian politics. It's ok to say that you're not the expert, but at least have a one-question-deep knowledge of related issues.

Sometimes you shouldn't answer a question.

Saying no is a perfectly acceptable response. Some situations and suggested responses include:

When you are the wrong person. You may be asked a question during a briefing that is outside of your account, on a topic unrelated to your briefing, or on an issue with which you are unfamiliar. Try responding with:

> "Jay here follows that issue closely. Jay, any thoughts?" (Of course, work out with Jay ahead of time that you'll funnel these questions to him before the briefing, or you may find yourself looking for a ride back to the office!)

> "This question focuses on an issue covered by my colleague, Cindy. I'm sure she can provide some insights. I can contact her as soon as I return to my office to ensure you get a response. Would this be acceptable?"

Classification. If asked a question that requires responding with classified information beyond the level for which the audience is cleared, declining to respond is clear-cut since the reason for saying "no" is due to circumstances outside your control. Try responding with:

> "My understanding of what you are asking is based on classified information. Since this is an unclassified briefing, I'm afraid I really can't get into that right now."

> "Unfortunately, our information on that matter is classified at a level beyond this briefing. I'm not authorized to discuss that right now."

If appropriate, you may be able to offer a separate, classified briefing, or suggest preparing a written response for delivery to an individual with the proper clearances.

Use this technique sparingly. You often can provide a less-sensitive answer that will satisfy the principal. Hearing "I know something you don't know, and I'm not telling" is never welcome.

Policy Prescription. Sometimes, consumers will ask for your opinion on policy courses of action. If you are strictly providing an informational briefing, you should avoid offering opinions. You are in the room as a representative of your organization. Even when pressed for "oh, just give me your opinion," don't take the bait. If you are not briefing someone directly in your food chain, do not offer opinions. Even providing a hint that you have opinions on legal decisions, policy, or similar issues and are willing to share them may compel some customers to keep asking for more, often pulling you down a very difficult path.

Consider the *Washington Post* test: Do you want your answer, attributed to you, appearing in tomorrow's edition? As soon as you sense that a customer is asking for your thoughts or opinions on particular courses of action, your best bet is to quickly move the conversation away from policy and back to an objective briefing on the topic at hand. Try responding with:

> "Clearly, legal decisions or policy on this matter can be complex. However, my job is to provide an explanation of the information and how we see the issue developing. I defer to you on what policy on the situation should look like. So, as I was saying…"

A political minefield. There are times when an audience member—including some policymakers—try to "score points" by goading a briefer to answer a question that supports one side over another on an issue. This frequently happens during congressional testimony. Sometimes a Member is merely garbing a political point in the clothing of a question, but doesn't really expect you to answer it. It is these questions to which it is most difficult to say no.

Savvy decision-makers are good at asking questions that they know to be within your realm of expertise and not policy prescriptive, eliminating all excuses for you to provide an answer. They also can phrase the question in a manner that will hem in the briefer in terms of his/her ability to answer. For example:

> "Wouldn't you agree that the Ruritanians have no other choice but to take a stand, especially after they've been hounded by the administration while doing absolutely nothing objectionable in their eyes? What other options do they have?"

Listen for the phrase "wouldn't you agree"—nothing good ever follows it! A close cousin is "If I understand what you're saying…" Make sure that they really are summarizing what you just said, rather than creating a caricature.

In such cases, your best course of action may be to acknowledge the value of such a question yet also defer answering it. This can take the form of openly dissecting the question and addressing only one aspect of it. Try responding with:

> "We do not have any information concerning the Ruritanians regarding this matter, which is clearly a delicate situation." Then present a review of what the media's interpretations are and what the realities are, or whatever other pertinent information you may have. You'll quickly find yourself in trouble if you hint that you agree with the customer, "Well, I think that this is because…"

If questioner persists in trying to bait you, stick to your script and stay with the prepared portions of your briefing. Sometimes acknowledging directly that you are feeling uncomfortable with the line of questioning can work. Try responding with:

> "I'm sorry but this is the extent of the reporting we have on this topic. Turning to the other agenda items, I'd like to pick up where I left off…"

> "I wonder if we could follow up on this after I complete the additional points that I prepared for you. I notice that we're now quite pressed for time."

You eventually will face **other types of questions,** including hostile, left-field, dumb, and inarticulate ones. Let's take them in turn.

Hostile questions can be similar to those we've just reviewed, but delivered with an emotional and sometimes high-decibel-laden edge to them. A few things to keep in mind:

- Don't take challenging questions personally. Keep a thick skin.

- The questioner may have an agenda that has nothing to do with you, and the question is aimed at the ears of someone else in the room.

- Avoid snapping back at the individual, which can cost you the support of the audience—many of whom are just as irritated with the individual as you are.

- Be polite and firm. You are likely to have to say no more than once.

- Don't apologize for your inability to answer a question. Simply state that you are not in a position to discuss the question, and move on.

- Don't be embarrassed or flustered. Customers usually appreciate an honest response and will respect you for it.

- Never make up an answer for a question you cannot address. Do not "wing it."

- If providing a good answer means collaborating with other colleagues in your organization, do so.

Questions from Left Field, Dumb Questions, and Inarticulately-Posed Questions are a triumvirate of troubles that can easily be mishandled. Remember that the principal comes from a different environment than you, and has other things on his/her mind. It may well be that your statement triggers what in their minds is a related issue, but doesn't sound like that to you. They may not have the knowledge base that you have.

Naiveté and ignorance does not mean stupidity. Always respect the questioner and the question.

By the way, please do *not* observe, "**that's a good question**," even if it is. This can be misinterpreted by a well-meaning, or hostile, audience. The straphangers in the room can hear "the other questions I've been asked were posed by losers." One member of Congress once responded to this well-meaning "good question" with "let me remind you that you are here to answer my questions, not evaluate them." Stick to the answer, and if you need to tap dance, don't use the "good question" phrase to stall for time. If you need to pause to collect your thoughts, then pause, period. If you need to fill, try "that's an issue with which we've been wrestling." This phrasing brings the principal into the intellectual boat with you, adding to their feeling of ownership of the briefing. They're now part of the in-group.

Staying on Topic

In a typical briefing, the discussion can get off topic. While you want to be responsive to the needs of your audience by answering questions as they arise—do not put them off—you also want to be sure that you cover the material that they need to hear. You can always try the rhetorical trick: "That leads us to…" your next point.

Here are a few *Common Situations*:

Competing with Recent Events. If a significant event has occurred just before your briefing, attendees may be more interested in it than the issues that you are prepared to discuss. In this situation, it is critical to consider how the event might affect what you planned to present. It is also critical to have the latest on it—even if it has absolutely nothing to do with your original topic. Make sure to be up-to-the-minute on your topic. Read the news media to which your audience attends, listen to radio news on the drive over, ask the staffers what topics they're working on when you arrive. They see you as The Expert on this topic, and will look to you for insights on a fast-breaking issue. For example:

> "I prepared my briefing for you before this recent event, so while I have some details on it, any comments I have are preliminary in nature and do not reflect the input of colleagues with possibly greater expertise than I can offer on this topic."

Competing Agendas/Personalities. Competing agendas exist in both the legislative and executive branches of government and certainly in boardrooms. One reason a policymaker may have requested a briefing is to help buttress his/her own viewpoint. While this may not be as common in the field, do not overlook the possibility of such an eventuality, especially with local, state, or other external organizations with whom you regularly deal.

Hijacking. The communities we brief include some forceful personalities. One or more attendees may try to take over your briefing with pointed questions as a way to push a personal agenda. Again, try "that leads me to" and return to your talking points' order.

Tangential issues. You may touch on a topic that sparks a tangential discussion that can take you away from your main briefing topic.

Common Solutions

Depending on the reason for the interruption, a variety of responses can work well:

- "Given the time we have today, I'm not certain that we can cover your many questions as well as the issue you earlier asked me to discuss. How would you like to proceed?"

- "My understanding is that you wished me to discuss topic X but your interest seems focused on topic Y. Should we plan another meeting so that I can prepare appropriately?"

- "I suggest taking a minute to examine fully the available material on the topic and then continue this discussion."

- "Are there questions from any others in the room?"

If you nonetheless are dragged off topic and time is waning, you can always use, "I'd be remiss if I didn't leave you with the following takeaway…"

We've covered a lot of ground in this chapter. I'd be remiss if I didn't ask: any questions!? :-)

■ Speaking Styles and Habits: Delivery

A litany of speaking quirks can derail an otherwise strong substantive presentation. In this chapter we will strive to pare down unforced/unintentional/unawareness errors, allow you to consider what you like and don't like in a speaker, and how you can use this information to improve your presentations. We'll also examine how speaker characteristics—verbal and nonverbal—affect how a message is received.

What makes an effective speaker? We've already talked about how to tailor material for an audience, and how to organize it most effectively. In this chapter, we're going to look at the delivery system—you—and how you can avoid bad habits and be even more effective as a briefer.

Let's take a look at what makes an effective speaker/briefer, and what detracts from presentations. Let's first look at speakers that you've liked. Name who you consider to be good speakers.

Looking at the speakers on this list, what is it that they do that led you to list them? What qualities do they have in common? Or perhaps only one of them has this quality. What do you like about them? What did they do that worked?

Now let's consider speakers that you haven't found effective. You can name them, or just think about generically bad speakers. What qualities (if disqualities isn't a word, it should be!) do they lack? They might include: engaged, natural, energetic, credible, knowledgeable, concise, clear, relevant, prepared, and professional.

That's quite a list of do's and don't's. But keep in mind that what works for others won't necessarily work for you. Don't mimic.

Let's take a look at a few speech tics that you'll want to purge from your style.

First, **uptalk**? It's putting a higher-pitched lilt at the end of a sentence, making it sound like a question. It occurs in men and women. Linguists trace it from the West Coast and believe it might have started in the 1970s/1980s. It's since metastasized across the country, firmly landing comfortably on the East Coast. It's commonly found among Generation Ys, although younger Gen Xrs also speak it.

What do you think of the speaker when you hear uptalk? Ditzy? Unsure of themselves? Unpolished? Uptalk can easily undercut the effectiveness of your message, morphing a strong declarative sentence into a mincing question. It can sound wishy-washy and obsequious, undercutting clarity, confidence, and authority. The sentence is now burdened with an implied "I hope you're buying what I'm saying" or "I hope you understood what I just said. Please ask for clarification if you didn't understand something." All this with a simple lilt on the final syllable before a sentence's period!

Why do speakers do this? It might not just be that they're mimicking each other. Some researchers suggest that it's designed to soften a self-perceived harshness. If so, it oversucceeds.

How can you protect yourself against this? One way is to record your briefing, and listen to it. Another is to listen to the Washington Drop, which is designed to give people the impression that you're fully in charge of the words you're saying, and that you're saying them with conviction, whether real or imagined. A past master of this technique is President Obama... who boldfaces... every verb... and noun... in his sentences... and hits a downbeat... at the end of his declarative statements. William Shatner used an early form of the Drop in the late 1960s when he portrayed Captain James... Tiberius... Kirk.

A second and somewhat newer popular verbal tic is **glottalization**—is that a great word or what?—more commonly known as **vocal frying**, which entails fluttering your vocal cords. It was first discovered in 1964 among upper-class British men saying 'n'yeeessss," and has recently been seen in Gen Ys trying to sound chic.

Third, well, so, if you will, in a manner of speaking, let's sort of look at, like, other, um, I'm like, and then he goes, verbal tics, known as **verbal graffiti**. How often have you heard such filler words? The ones I threw out there—and there are tons of others—are ones you commonly hear from Americans. Filler words differ across cultures. Israelis tend to "eh", Canadians tend to "A".

Why do people use fillers? They are not on their talking points (or scripts, if they, ugh, try to memorize their presentation. As an aside, **do not** memorize (except for your opening 3 sentences to establish eye contact). If you're asked a question, it'll throw you off your line of march. And if you suddenly lose your place, you'll increase your nervousness as you strain to remember your next line. On the other hand, do not walk in with no notes. I guarantee: you'll forget something. Always have the notes with you, even if you don't look down to refer to them. It'll increase your confidence, and look to the principal like you're not just winging it. Now back to our show.).

Fillers—no matter what their length—serve a useful, if unintentional, purpose. They fill in the silent void whenever we're searching for a word or a thought. Americans are especially leery of conversational or monologue silences, and will do anything they can to wrestle one to the floor and pin it down. It comes from our listening to the radio. When you get radio silence, what do you do? Turn to another station, right? We subconsciously fear that the audience will tune us out if they hear a silence.

Surprisingly, **pauses** are your friend. Although you've heard—at least in your head—the thoughts you're expressing, your audience has never heard it put in quite that way. The pause lets the audience catch up to you intellectually, allowing them to process what you just said. It also gives them the unarticulated message that you're not just rambling on, but are carefully choosing just the right words to convey your message.

Finally, you can use the pause when you want to involve the audience in a discussion. After you ask a question to which you really want an answer (not just a rhetorical question), pause 7 seconds. The silence is excruciating to Americans, and *someone* in the audience will say *something* just to relieve the tension. A past master of this technique is former President Bill Clinton, who, when hearing a question, walks 2 steps toward the questioner and asks, "by the way, what was your name?" Whether it's a softball question or one coming between his eyes, it gives him the 3-4 seconds he needs to compose himself and think of an answer. It works for him and it can work for you.

Crutch words are similar to verbal graffiti. "You know" has retired the crutch word trophy, but you'll hear others as well, basically, like, if you will, ok.

Another variant of verbal graffiti is found in the "**sorta**" "kinda" family. These terms drain the declarative sentence of its strength. They are commonly found in conversation, but should be eliminated in briefings. If you are not 100% sure of your judgments, state that uncertainty as such. "Kinda" can mean anywhere from 1% to 100%, and therefore means nothing. Martin Luther King didn't "sorta have a dream." Caesar didn't "came, saw, and sorta conquered." Neither should you.

How do you stop the onslaught of verbal graffiti? One way is to simply close your mouth when you feel one coming on. You can't say it if your lips are sealed! You can also listen to yourself on tape; it'll help you spot the fillers. It takes practice, but you can eliminate them, one um at a time. If you cannot find the word, embrace the pause. Look at the forehead of someone in the 3rd row from the back. They'll think that you're giving them special attention, and I guarantee, you will find that word.

Remember to **slow down**. Not everything needs to be Aaron Sorkin-speed quips.

Fourth, **jargon**, its rich cousin **acronyms**, and its poor cousin, **slanguage**, force the audience to translate what you just said into more understandable language. Jargon exists in any professional group, and is used to establish in-group membership and provides a shorthand language to speed up communication amongst experts. No need to use it here. Similarly, acronyms are a clipped way of communicating between the cognoscenti, but are barriers to communicating with anyone else.

Slang is just a bad habit. I'm like: Don't use it, dude.

If you are going to use a **translator** with an audience and must use specialized language, make sure you point out these terms to the translator beforehand. If you must use an acronym or jargon, make sure that the translator understands the nuance of the term. President Carter thought he told the Poles "I embrace your principles" but the translator told them "I want to embrace you carnally." This came after his *Playboy* interview, so maybe the translator was thinking… Speaking of, and with, translators, make sure you go slowly so that the translator has time to catch up. Pausing at each comma in your sentence helps tremendously.

Fifth, although I can't believe I need to say this, do not use **profanity**, even if the principal uses it with you or his/her colleagues. We are *among* the customers, not *of* them. Just because they drop an F-bomb does not mean that we have license for massive retaliation.

Make sure you're **pronouncing** words correctly. Avoid regionalisms. Look for jawbreakers in your notes, and find unfamiliar words. Make sure you know the correct pronunciation of foreign words. Knowledgeable principals who have worked in the region will tune you out—and maybe call you out—for such bloopers. Mispronunciation is a very simple way to lose the assumption of competence regarding your expertise.

Your toolkit has more than just your words to get your point across. You also have **gestures, facial expressions**, and **vocal variety**. All three of these can increase the apparent energy of your presentation, making you more interesting, and possibly entertaining, as a speaker. Use them. In addition to pauses being your friend, this trinity is also your friend. Ignore anyone who says that gestures are unprofessional. This advice is given by boring speakers. If you're not a natural gesture machine, just try out one or two, but make sure that they come out naturally. Try out the gestures while you're practicing the words; get them to sync. Same for facial expressions—the facial cousin of gestures—and other body language. We're hardwired to pick up these subtle cues. Use them to your advantage.

Tics—verbal and physical—are not your friend. Watch the tape to find them, then eliminate them.

Be aware of what certain gestures mean in different cultures. In the US, an index finger means One. In Germany, it means Two—the thumb is assumed. This can get you in trouble if you think you ordered One beer in a bar. That index finger can also be used as a pointer. But some people bristle at being pointed at, subconsciously viewing it as a gun (the fist, and the cocked thumb are assumed) aimed at them. Airline flight attendants now point with all of their fingers straightened together, not just with the single digit. President Bill Clinton changed his index finger pointer to his thumb, which also subtly gives a "thumbs up". What are your gestures unintentionally saying?

Vocal variety comes in several flavors—volume, tempo, pitch, tone.

Make sure you can be heard. It doesn't matter if you are the greatest analyst in the world—if they can't hear you, your message is lost. Practice with an audience, not just a mirror. If you see them straining, get louder. Speak from your diaphragm. A speech coach, drama coach, or singing instructor can help you. I'm not advocating your Taking Over the Room by dialing up the decibels, just that you can be heard. (By the way, when you're researching the principal, make sure to determine whether they have 100% of their hearing. Sometimes principals will turn their good ear towards you. This can be misinterpreted as them turning away from you. They're just trying to take in what you have to say.)

Regarding how to master diaphragmatic breathing/projection, clinical psychologist Dr. Robi Tarmargo suggests using the same wind-generation technique as you use in blowing bubbles from a child's bubblemaker toy. It comes from the diaphragm, not the throat or the mouth.

Speaking of volume, if there's a **microphone** in the room, use it. It doesn't matter if you're a Juilliard-trained Shakespearean actor who projects to the back of the hall, use the microphone—it is less tiring to your voicebox than projecting or yelling. Projecting comes from your diaphragm; yelling comes from your voicebox. The first is a Good Thing; the second just wears out you and your audience.

- Try out the mic you'll be using and make sure that your mouth is the proper distance from it. Some mics have a very broad pickup, and 4 inches away is fine. Others require a 1 inch distance from your mouth.

- If using a handheld mic, gesture only with the hand not holding the mic. You'll otherwise lose the volume boost from the mic, and just look silly.

- Do not blow or tap on the mic to determine whether it is working. It is a delicate instrument, and you can unintentionally damage it. What's a mic for? Speaking! So speak into it! Say something like, "can everyone hear me," which also focuses the audience's attention into the presentation.

- Don't speak directly into the mic; speak a few degrees away from a straight line at the mic. This will prevent explosives, such as words beginning with P, from bursting into the mic.

Once again, slow down. Your nervousness will make you unintentionally speed up. You can write little pauses into your text. Don't articulate "pause here"! Simple yellow highlights that mean "slow down" also mean that you need to process fewer words from your notes.

Pitch can also be controlled. High pitchy voices, in addition to annoying Simon Cowell, are difficult to listen to for a sustained period. As we get more nervous, our vocal cords seize up, increasing the high pitch. Morgan Freeman, often referred to as the Voice of God, suggests yawning, often, to relax your vocal cords. (As we said in our chapter on nervousness, yawn before the briefing.) That relaxation also deepens your pitch. We're not going to start a new religion based upon your vocal cords, but it can help with your pitch.

Tone can underscore key words. Unlike written text, in which you can use color, underscores, italics, boldface, and font changes, our voice has to do the work. A monotone will quickly lose the most rapt of audiences. Use tone changes for emphasis.

Finally, consider your overall **presence**, which derives from your confidence, eye contact, posture and dress.

You're looking to project an image of your certainty that this is the best briefing they can get anywhere on this topic. Never apologize—for having a cold, the temperature in the room, the readability of your slides, or whatever else. It undermines your credibility. They are thinking about themselves, not you. Be confident, and show it.

What's the key to message delivery? Psycholinguist Alfred Mehrabian says that when an audience is evaluating a speaker's likeability (not the message itself, which is a frequent misinterpretation of his study) and responding to the speaker emotionally, 55% is attributable to body language, 38% to voice/tone, and only 7% to the actual words.

What this means for you is: Don't read from your notes verbatim, but it's ok to look down at them when you need to find your next thought. You're briefing the *person*, not the *notes*. Don't stare down the principal. Your eye contact should be the length of a handshake. After that, move your eyes to the next person in the room. You can break the room into 3 zones, dividing your eye contact between them. Look mostly at the principal, but don't forget the straphangers. Your eye contact generates sincerity and credibility.

If using slides, talk to the audience; don't turn your back on them to read the slides—that's what your notes pages are for.

Regarding **posture**, if you're standing, place your heels directly under your shoulders, and stand erect. Do not shift your weight from side to side, or the audience will become distracted by the breathing metronome in front of them. If you look confident, you'll feel confident and project that image to the room.

Dress for what's appropriate for the room for a briefer. Do not dress to distract, intentionally or unintentionally. The audience expects professionalism in their briefers, no matter what they happen to be wearing (my colleagues and I have briefed seniors in their jammies, in shorts, in jeans, in overalls—again, we're among them, but not of them.) Wear professionally neutral garb. No shiny or large objects, no flashy patterns, no idiosyncratic ties. If you're seated, no heavy cufflinks or other clunky jewelry that can loudly clack on the table. Some organizations fancifully suggest that you should only have 7 items of bling (including belt buckles, watches, necklaces, lapel pins, broaches, earrings, tats). If it is possible for the eyes or ears to wander, they will. Remember, the audience is probably of a certain age, and has expectations of briefers that are probably more conservative than that of the general population. Don't distract them by unintentionally irritating them with hidden messages in your clothing choices. When you practice, practice in the clothes you'll be wearing for the briefing. You'll feel differently in "game-worn" apparel.

When you're practicing, also practice gestures and other nonverbals, including tone and pitch. Most briefers practice only the words. Be the briefer they remember, give them the message they remember, by practicing the entire package.

■ Group Briefings

In this chapter, we'll examine how best to organize a group briefing and develop strategies for deconflicting and creating Plan B for hiccups that might arise.

Sometimes you're the key expert on a topic, sometimes others are needed to provide context, seniority, clout, entrée, or expertise on topics related to yours.

Preparing a group briefing should involve everyone, so that all agree on the overall message being delivered. There are two basic ways to handle a team briefing.

Single Briefer: One person delivers the briefing based on the work of all team members. The individual team members usually answer the questions, rather than the singleton spokesperson. This can vary with the relative seniority of the briefing team. In some organizations, the junior team members are there to provide the singleton briefer with backup material as needed, but do not directly answer the question.

Specialized Briefers: Each member of the team briefs on his/her specialization. The briefers must relate to each other and the overall theme and conclusions and should work out the general themes of the briefing, who does what, and who will serve as the traffic cop for doling out questions.

What types of things can go wrong during multi-briefer briefings? Three stand out:

- **Ball hogging:** How often have you had a partner dominate the briefing time, cutting into the time you thought you had agreed you'd have, and forcing you to edit your presentation on the fly? Be sure to work out this issue with your partner(s), and look to your "traffic cop" team member if your colleague drones on and on.

- **Partner provides wrong information:** This can be tricky to correct. You might use a formulation like "there are several interpretations of the data, one of which Jim has just outlined for you. Others include… On balance, we find compelling the following one."

- **Partner(s) do not arrive on time, or never arrive:** Traffic happens. Emergencies happen. Be sure that you have copies of everyone's material—handouts, slides, props, and anything else, and reorganize the briefing so that those who are there go first, hoping that the no-shows eventually arrive. If you can cover your missing-in-action colleagues' material, do so. If not, offer to the audience an opportunity to reschedule.

Of course, there are always personality clashes, bureaucratic infighting, and the like, which can become part of the landscape of multi-briefer briefing preparation and presentation. Those crop up in most every professional environment. There are no simple solutions, and the techniques of organizational psychology are beyond the scope of this handbook.

■ Follow-up

After you've met with the principal, what comes next? You need to have an after-action plan, identifying individuals who have a stake in the briefing and determine whether you need to inform them of how the briefing went, what remains to be done, and anything else that affects their equities. It's not just the people in the briefing room who have a rooting interest in how the briefing goes; there are usually multiple players involved, directly and indirectly.

You've driven back from the scene of the crime (um, briefing), and returned to your desk. It's all over, right? Not quite so. It ain't over until:

- It's over –Yogi Berra, 1973
- The Fat Lady Sings –Washington Bullets, 1978
- The paperwork is done.
- You've taken care of a few post-briefing obligations.

You're not the only person interested in the outcome of your briefing. Who else might be interested? To focus your list-making, ask yourself:

- Who in your foodchain needs to know what?

- Does anyone outside of your management have an interest?

- What does each of them need to know, and how quickly?

- Is there a briefing knowledge base to which you can contribute?

- If things went badly, report out immediately. It's always best that the interested party hears your side of the story first. Whom do you tell? In what format—in person, email, instant message, memo, database entry?

In our discussion of Questions, we noted that you should always write down—in front of the principal, during the briefing—a question they asked that you promised to answer downstream. It doesn't matter how smart you think you are, or what memory tricks you have, in the heat of the moment, you're going to forget at least one of those questions. There's nothing like having to go back to the principal—if that's even possible—after the briefing, perhaps days after, to ask them to repeat the question. There is no upside to having to do this. So write it down. It sends them the message that you're taking their question seriously, and that they can count on you getting back to them with an answer. If they asked just out of curiosity or to keep up their end of the conversation, they'll tell you. If the question is important to them, they'll also let you know.

Make sure you provide what you promised to the briefee. If you promised something to be delivered by a colleague or other organization, give them a heads-up immediately.

Here's a short checklist for you. Add to it as appropriate for your environment:

What explicit followup requests were made– and to which you agreed?

- What was requested?

- How did you reply?

- Who needs to develop the response? Will they also need to deliver it, or will you be the follow-up deliverer?

- When is it expected?

- Who needs to know it is being done?

- What's the chain of review? How long will that delay delivery of the response?

- Does a graphics shop, print shop, or other service organization need to massage the material?

Were any implicit followup requests made?

- Based upon the "feel" you developed during the briefing for the needs of the principal, are there any analytic opportunities—papers or additional briefings—that you, your team, or a fellow team—could provide?

- Is a paper or briefing required to address issues where clarification and/or further research is needed?

- Do you need to disseminate what was just delivered elsewhere?

- Did the principal request/suggest that you brief his/her colleagues/seniors?

- Are you in a position to quickly organize a follow-up briefing at a lower level—and perhaps at an unclassified level for press or foreign partners? If not you, then who?

What did you learn?

- What new information/analysis/insight was acquired from the principal?

- From others in the room?
- From the moat monster?
- Did you discover a different reason for you to be in the room, briefing on that topic, which aims you in a new direction in understanding the customer's analytic/informational needs?
- What did you learn about the principal?
- What would you do differently the next time you brief this principal? What heads-up will you give to your successor as a briefer?
- How are decisionmakers collaborating/battling on this issue?
- What coalitions are emerging?
- Which organizations are the dissenters?
- What opportunities are there for briefing others in the principal's inner circle, as well as outside the principal's organization?
- What US foreign and domestic policy and/or commercial equities are influencing policy?
- Which decisionmakers are driving the policy?
- How might your organization's analysis be misrepresented/misinterpreted/leaked by any of these actors?

Who needs to know about this—and when—and in what format?

- Managers
- Other analysts
- Collectors
- Inspector General/other specialized offices
- Law enforcement

Finally, think about your own equities and personal/professional growth:

- How did you perform as a briefer/substantive expert?
- What did you learn about yourself?
- How could you improve?

■ Practice Exercise

It's now time for you to put it all together, giving yourself the opportunity to develop confidence, learn from others, and try new techniques. There's only so much you can learn from talking to a mirror. Taping and watching your briefings with others, with color commentary by you, colleagues, and managers will help you identify your briefing strengths (and believe me, you have them, despite your being your severest critic!) and spot areas for development, improvement, and experimentation.

There are two schools on evaluating: One embraces checklists that can go on for pages. The checklists can have a Likert scale, and/or a narrative section (the latter is far more helpful, when specific comments are offered, than is "I gave it a 5, it was easy to dance to and I liked the beat."). Here's a very simple evaluation form. Include whatever you find helpful:

Briefing Critique

Briefer:

Evaluated by:

Subject:

Date:

1. Overall clarity of the briefing

    ▪ BLUF

    ▪ Roadmap

    ▪ Supporting evidence

    ▪ Alternative analysis

2. Eye contact/posture/body language/energy

3. Visual aids/graphics

4. Organization of the briefing

5. Question handling

6. General comments

Add to this as you see fit. You can also look to lists written by such groups as Toastmasters, who also have designated "um" counters.

Tape yourself giving a briefing, then watch the briefing all the way through. Do not stop-motion it to say "I should have moved my hand 3 inches higher and 13 degrees to the right to emphasize this word." Try to get the overall feeling of the briefing, as it was experienced by the audience. Then move to what the FBI calls the "praise and polish" sequence. First, the briefer will explain what they liked about their performance. Let me repeat—liked. It is too easy to immediately jump into "I was terrible" litanies. First concentrate on what worked for you. Then ask your colleagues to point out what strengths they saw in the briefing. After that, return to the briefer, who will examine what areas s/he would like to develop/change/experiment with, given what they saw on the tape. Colleagues will then also offer suggestions.

After you try this, consider this key takeaway: you are a better briefer than you give yourself credit for. While your little voice inside your head is yelling "You stink! You said 'um'. You forgot a point! You didn't give the points in the line of march you'd prepared!", the audience doesn't know any of this. The audience simply knows that a competent briefing is being given, and they're getting what they need.

Now go forward and give great briefings!

■ Bibliography

I could burden you with hundreds of citations on the topics we've covered. But in the spirit of being brief, let's just look at the few that you really should check out.

Nervousness

Timothy J. Koegel *The Exceptional Presenter: A Proven Formula to Open Up and Own the Room* Austin, Texas: Greenleaf Book Group Press, 2007, 188 pp.

Maura Rhodes "Fears 2015" *Parade Magazine* January 18, 2015, pp. 4-8

Laura Vanderkam "The Introvert on the Podium" *New York Times*, November 23, 2014, p. 10

Organizing a Briefing

Chip Heath and Dan Heath *Made to Stick: Why Some Ideas Thrive and Others Die* New York: Random House, 2007, 291 pp. A one-page summary is available at http://heathbrothers.com/download/mts-made-to-stick-model.pdf

Graphics

Garr Reynolds *Presentation Zen: Simple Ideas on Presentation Design and Delivery* San Francisco: New Riders, 2008, 229 pp.

Edward R. Tufte *Beautiful Evidence* Cheshire, Connecticut: Graphics Press, 2006

Edward R. Tufte *The Cognitive Style of PowerPoint* Cheshire, Connecticut: Graphics Press, 2003

Edward R. Tufte *Envisioning Information* Cheshire, Connecticut: Graphics Press, 2001

Edward R. Tufte, *The Visual Display of Quantitative Information*, 2nd ed. Cheshire, Connecticut: Graphics Press, 2001

Edward R. Tufte *Visual Explanations: Images and Quantities, Evidence and Narrative* Cheshire, Connecticut: Graphics Press, 1997

Speaking Styles

Jargonator column in *Ink Magazine*

Steven Kurutz "The 'Kind of, Sort Of' Era" *New York Times*, November 2, 2014, p. 12

Edward Mickolus and Joseph Brannan *Coaching Winning Model United Nations Teams: A Teacher's Guide* Washington, DC: Potomac Books, 2013

Ken White "Tips for Improving Your Public Speaking" Washington Post Career Coach WashingtonPost.com/capital_business

Videos

You'll find it helpful to watch these videos while absorbing the material in their accompanying chapters. Some things you just have to see and/or hear to appreciate, such as uptalk and vocal frying.

Nervousness

Free visualization audios at http://www.helpguide.org/articles/stress/relaxation-techniques-for-stress-relief.htm

Know Your Audience

"Call me Senator" video
https://youtu.be/f0CprVYsG0k

Graphics

How Steve Jobs did it:
https://youtu.be/RHX-xnP_G5s

Don McMillan on How not to use Powerpoint:
https://youtu.be/lpvgfmEU2Ck

Answering Questions

Miss Teen South Carolina Caitlin Upton answers a question:
https://youtu.be/lj3iNxZ8Dww

Miss Utah answers a question:
https://youtu.be/8kgL84uTRWA

Rep. Hank Johnson asks a question on Guam's tipping point:
https://www.youtube.com/watch?v=bs23CjIWMgA

"The front fell off" Q&A
https://www.youtube.com/watch?v=8bqTBh1yxbM

Speaking Styles

Uptalk

Taylor Mali on uptalk:
https://www.youtube.com/watch?v=SCNIBV87wV4
A graphics version of his presentation is available at
https://www.youtube.com/watch?v=OEBZkWkkdZA

What is uptalk:
https://youtu.be/HEfMwri22SM

Vocal Frying

Vocal frying by a woman:
https://www.youtube.com/watch?v=YEqVgtLQ7qM

Howard Stern shows how it sounds in a male voice:
https://www.youtube.com/watch?v=4iyJmpxtZDE

Psycholinguistics of vocal fry/uptalk among professional women: https://www.youtube.com/watch?v=w7BBNEwyOjw

Vocal Fry News:
https://www.youtube.com/watch?v=KHeecOiWHyM

Rambling

"The Office'"s Michael Scott on rambling:
Youtube.com/watch?v=caTXTU5tqs at 40 seconds

■ About the Author

Dr. Edward Mickolus, after graduating from Georgetown University, wrote the first doctoral dissertation on international terrorism while earning an M.A., M.Phil, and Ph.D. from Yale University.

He then served in analytical, operational, management, and staff positions in the Central Intelligence Agency for 33 years, where he was CIA's first full-time analyst on international terrorism; analyzed African political, economic, social, military, and leadership issues; wrote political-psychological assessments of world leaders; and managed collection, counterintelligence, and covert action programs against terrorists, drug traffickers, weapons proliferators, and hostile espionage services.

He founded Vinyard Software, Inc., (https://www.vinyardsoftware.com/) whose products include ITERATE (International Terrorism: Attributes of Terrorist Events) text and numeric datasets and DOTS (Data on Terrorist Suspects). Clients include 200 universities in two dozen countries.

His 40 books include a series of multi-volume chronologies and biographies on international terrorism; more than two dozen book chapters; 100 articles and reviews in refereed scholarly journals and newspapers and presentations to professional societies; and 14 humorous publications.

For the following ten years, he was a senior instructor for SAIC and its spinoff, Leidos, Inc. He served as the Deborah M. Hixon Professor of Intelligence Tradecraft and Board of Advisors member at the Daniel Morgan Graduate School in Washington, D.C. and teaches at the University of North Florida and Jacksonville University.

Books by Ed Mickolus

America's Funniest Memes: Coronavirus Edition

More Stories From Langley: Another Glimpse Inside the CIA

Terrorism Worldwide, 2018

His Words

The Secret Book of Intelligence Community Humor

Two Spies Walk Into a Bar

Terrorism Worldwide, 2017

Terrorism Worldwide, 2016

Terrorism 2013-2015: A Worldwide Chronology

Briefing for the Boardroom and the Situation Room

The Counterintelligence Chronology: Spying by and Against the United States from the 1700s through 2014

Food with Thought: The Wit and Wisdom of Chinese Fortune Cookies

Stories from Langley: A Glimpse Inside the CIA

with Susan L. Simmons *The 50 Worst Terrorist Attacks*

Terrorism 2008-2012: A Worldwide Chronology

with Joseph T. Brannan *Coaching Winning Model United Nations Teams*

The Secret Book of CIA Humor

with Susan L. Simmons *The Terrorist List: North America*

with Susan L. Simmons *The Terrorist List: South America*

with Susan L. Simmons *The Terrorist List: Eastern Europe*

with Susan L. Simmons *The Terrorist List: Western Europe*

with Susan L. Simmons *The Terrorist List: Asia, Pacific, and Sub-Saharan Africa*

The Terrorist List: The Middle East, 2 volumes

Terrorism, 2005-2007

with Susan L. Simmons *Terrorism, 2002-2004: A Chronology*, 3 volumes

with Susan L. Simmons *Terrorism, 1996-2001: A Chronology of Events and a Selectively Annotated Bibliography*, 2 volumes

with Susan L. Simmons *Terrorism, 1992-1995: A Chronology of Events and a Selectively Annotated Bibliography*

Terrorism, 1988-1991: A Chronology of Events and a Selectively Annotated Bibliography

with Todd Sandler and Jean Murdock *International Terrorism in the 1980s: A Chronology, Volume 2: 1984-1987*

with Todd Sandler and Jean Murdock *International Terrorism in the 1980s: A Chronology, Volume 1: 1980-1983*

with Peter Flemming *Terrorism, 1980-1987: A Selectively Annotated Bibliography*

International Terrorism: Attributes of Terrorist Events, 1968-1977, ITERATE 2 Data Codebook

The Literature of Terrorism: A Selectively Annotated Bibliography

Transnational Terrorism: A Chronology of Events, 1968-1979

ITERATE: International Terrorism: Attributes of Terrorist Events, Data Codebook

Combatting International Terrorism: A Quantitative Analysis

with Joseph Rendon *Take My Weight... Please!*

with Harlan Rector *I Matter: Finding Meaning in Your Life at Any Age, volume 1*

with Harlan Rector *I Matter Too: Finding Meaning in Your Life at Any Age, volume 2 (forthcoming)*

Terrorism Worldwide 2019-2020 (forthcoming)

More Funny 2020 Covid Memes (forthcoming)

with Tracy Tripp *White Noise Whispers*

Made in the USA
Columbia, SC
07 August 2021

43183529R00046